Oceans

SIMON & SCHUSTER BOOKS FOR YOUNG READERS
An imprint of Simon & Schuster Children's Publishing Division
1230 Avenue of the Americas, New York, New York 10020

Conceived and produced by Weldon Owen Pty Ltd
61 Victoria Street, McMahons Point
Sydney, NSW 2060, Australia

Group Chief Executive Officer John Owen
President and Chief Executive Officer Terry Newell
Publisher Sheena Coupe
Creative Director Sue Burk
Concept Development John Bull, The Book Design Company
Editorial Coordinator Mike Crowton
Vice President, International Sales Stuart Laurence
Vice President, Sales and New Business Development Amy Kaneko
Vice President, Sales: Asia and Latin America Dawn Low
Administrator, International Sales Kristine Ravn

Project Editor Jennifer Losco
Designer Dean Hudson, Burk Design
Cover Designers Gaye Allen and Kelly Booth

Color reproduction by Chroma Graphics (Overseas) Pte Ltd
Printed by SNP Leefung Printers Ltd
Manufactured in China

A WELDON OWEN PRODUCTION

SIMON & SCHUSTER BOOKS FOR YOUNG READERS is a trademark of Simon & Schuster, Inc.
The text for this book is set in Meta and Rotis Serif.
Cataloging-in-publication data for this book is available from the Library of Congress.

ISBN-13: 978-1-4169-6465-0
ISBN-10: 1-4169-6465-7

Oceans

Beverly McMillan and John A. Musick

Simon & Schuster Books for Young Readers
New York London Toronto Sydney

Contents

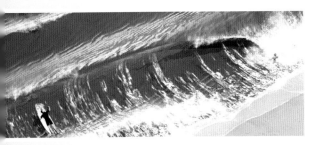

A Watery World

Our Extraordinary Blue Planet   8

The Formation of Earth's First Ocean   10

The Underwater Landscape   12

The Ocean in Motion   14

Oceans and Climate   16

Ocean Life

Regions and Zones: Ocean Habitats   18

Made for the Ocean: Adaptations   20

Great Ocean Migrations   22

Oceans Under Threat   24

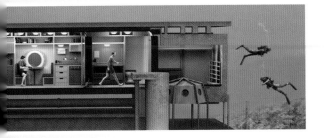

Exploring the Oceans

Deep-sea Legends   26

Highways for Exploration   28

Inside and Out: Galleon   30

The Ocean's Hidden Dangers   32

Exploring the Depths   34

The Ocean's Bounty   36

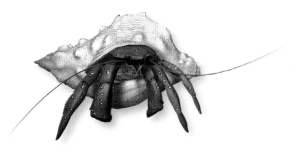

 *focus*

The Shallows

Exploring the Sandy Shore   40

Life Along the Rocky Shore   42

Estuaries   44

Abundance in the Coastal Sea   46

Colors of the Coral Reef   48

Hide-and-Seek in the Kelp Forest   50

Life in a World of Ice: Polar Seas   52

The Depths

Teeming with Life in the Sunlight Zone   54

Creatures of the Deep Sea   56

Life on the Ocean Floor: Hot Vents   58

Oceans of Wonder   60

Glossary   62

Index   64

introducing

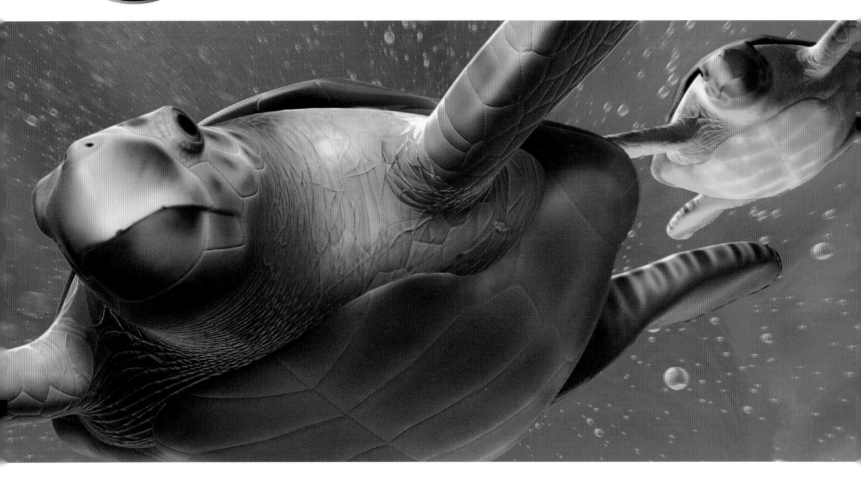

Our Extraordinary
Blue Planet

More than 70 percent of Earth's surface is liquid water, most of it in sparkling blue oceans. Seawater covers nearly 140 million square miles (361 million sq km) of Earth, a greater area than all the continents combined. The average ocean depth is 12,450 feet (3,796 m), which is equivalent to the height of 10 Empire State buildings, one on top of the other. Billions of years ago life began in the sea, and today it is home to countless animals, plants, and other forms of life. Ships travel the ocean carrying people and cargoes, and its waters provide us with food, minerals, and other products.

World ocean

There are five named oceans on Earth—the huge Pacific and Atlantic oceans, the Indian Ocean, the Southern Ocean, and the Arctic Ocean. Because these oceans are connected, they form a single world ocean. When an area of ocean is partly enclosed by land, it is called a sea.

Ocean sizes

Pacific Ocean
46% of the
world ocean

Atlantic Ocean
23% of the
world ocean

Indian Ocean
21% of the
world ocean

Arctic Ocean
4% of the
world ocean

Southern Ocean
6% of the
world ocean

Indian Ocean *The Indian Ocean extends from eastern Africa to Southeast Asia and Australia. It is the only ocean in which the currents switch direction—flowing toward Africa in winter and toward India in summer.*

Southern Ocean *The Southern Ocean surrounds icy Antarctica. In winter as much as 7.7 million square miles (20 million sq km) of this ocean is covered by ice.*

Our place from space
From space, Earth looks blue because the ocean covers so much of it. Clouds form when water evaporates from the sea.

Arctic Ocean *The Arctic Ocean is surrounded by land. Parts of it are always covered with ice. Earth's coldest ocean water is at the bottom of this ocean.*

Pacific Ocean *The Pacific is the largest and deepest ocean—it reaches almost halfway around Earth. The Pacific Ring of Fire, a zone that runs from New Zealand to southern Chile, experiences intense volcanic activity and violent earthquakes.*

Atlantic Ocean *The Atlantic Ocean stretches from the Americas to the west coasts of Europe and Africa. More of the world's large rivers, such as the Mississippi, the Amazon, and the Congo, flow into the Atlantic than into any other ocean.*

THE WATER CYCLE

Water evaporates from the sea and condenses to form cloud.

Rain falls from cloud.

Rivers drain into the ocean.

Inland water storages are refilled.

The water cycle provides Earth's supply of fresh water. Water that evaporates from the ocean falls as rain. Rivers carry some back to the sea, and some is stored in lakes and underground pools called aquifers.

Underground water returns to the ocean.

Ocean depths

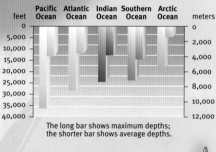

feet	Pacific Ocean	Atlantic Ocean	Indian Ocean	Southern Ocean	Arctic Ocean	meters
0						0
5,000						2,000
10,000						4,000
15,000						6,000
20,000						8,000
25,000						10,000
30,000						
35,000						12,000
40,000						

The long bar shows maximum depths; the shorter bar shows average depths.

Salty and fresh water

Less than 3 percent of Earth's water is found in rivers, lakes, groundwater, land ice, and vapor. The other 97 percent is salty seawater.

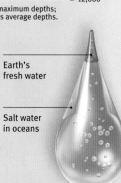

Earth's fresh water

Salt water in oceans

The Formation of Earth's
First Ocean

When Earth formed about 4.6 billion years ago, it was nothing like the planet we know today. Scientists believe the skinlike crust at Earth's surface was hot and rocky. Volcanoes erupted, lightning flashed, and dark clouds of gas and steam rose to the sky. Later, the first ocean began to form. According to theory, some of the water that filled this sea came from melting ice in comets and other material that bombarded the young planet from space. Much more fell as rain. By about 200 million years ago there was a single huge continent, which scientists now call Pangaea, surrounded by a vast ocean.

Earth's first atmosphere
Clouds of gas and water vapor formed Earth's first atmosphere. As the young planet cooled, the water vapor condensed into liquid water that fell as rain.

Earth's moving surface
Earth's crust is divided into sections called tectonic plates, outlined by red lines in the map below. Forces deep inside Earth move its plates. Earthquakes, tsunamis, and volcanic eruptions are triggered by these plate movements.

◀ ▶ Direction of plate movement

Oceans through time
Over time, continents move and ocean basins enlarge or shrink. Fifty million years from now, the Atlantic Ocean will be much wider than it is today.

200 million years ago
The world ocean surrounds a single huge continent, Pangaea.

90 million years ago
Moving plates split Pangaea and the Atlantic Ocean basin starts to form.

50 million years from now
Ocean basins change shape as plate movements continue.

Magma *The deeper parts of Earth's crust are hot, mudlike magma. When a volcano erupts, this fiery magma may rise to the surface and burst out along with steam and ash.*

Water cycle begins *Water evaporated from the ocean and other bodies of water, then fell back to Earth as rain. This was the start of Earth's water cycle.*

Salt for the ocean *Ash and other materials from early volcanoes contained chemicals, such as chloride and sulfide, that helped make the ocean salty.*

Birth of the ocean

When hot early Earth had cooled, steam from erupting volcanoes formed rain. The rainwater slowly filled low basins and washed minerals into them. After millions of years, seawater covered 70 percent of Earth's surface.

Islands are born *Movements of Earth's crustal plates pushed up new land areas. Like the water cycle, these processes go on today.*

Land and sea form *Some of Earth's crust remained as dry land while other parts sank and become the seafloor.*

THE DYNAMIC SEAFLOOR

Tectonic activity at mid-ocean ridges creates plates that form the seafloor. Earth's oceans are always on the move.

Seafloor spreading
Ocean plates move away from mid-ocean ridges where new crust is constantly being formed.

Spreading plate

Spreading plate

Ocean–continent collision
When an ocean plate slides under a continental plate, rising magma may form volcanoes and other mountains on land.

Magma pushing up volcano on land

Sinking ocean plate

Ocean–ocean collision
When one ocean plate slides under another one, magma may form volcanic islands that rise above the sea.

Sinking ocean plate

Soil and sediment *As rain fell over many millions of years, the land weathered and eroded. This created soil on land and sediments on the seafloor.*

Magma pushing up volcanoes in the ocean

The Underwater
Landscape

For thousands of years no one was able to examine what lay miles beneath the ocean's surface. With technology we now know that the ocean basins have features much like those on land. These include jagged mountain ranges; broad, smooth plains; deep canyons; and the tallest mountain on Earth–Hawaii. From its base on the floor of the Pacific Ocean to its snowy crest, the island of Hawaii, made from a volcano, is actually the world's tallest mountain. It measures 33,476 feet (10,203 m) tall–the equivalent of 33 Eiffel Towers stacked one on top of the other.

Measuring the deep
This array of scientific instruments will gather samples of microscopic organisms that live around hot springs on the ocean floor. Other instruments measure the chemical characteristics and the temperature of seawater at varying depths in the ocean.

Mapping the seafloor
Technicians use side-scan sonar to map the seafloor and search for sunken ships and planes.

Remote exploration
A technician in this vessel on the water's surface uses computer signals to control ROVs (remotely operated vehicles) and other instruments deep beneath the sea.

Hydrophone

Sound burst

Seismic surveying *Sound waves are used to study the inside of the seafloor. A burst of sound from an air gun or a small explosive travels down into the seabed. A hydrophone near the surface detects the echoes, which a computer aboard ship converts into an image.*

Sonar seafloor map
This sonar map of the seafloor off Los Angeles, USA, shows the sharp drop-off from the continental shelf to the continental slope.

1. **Side-scan sonar** *A side-scan sonar device sends out sound waves that bounce off objects and surfaces. Aboard ship, instruments convert these echoes into an image of the underwater world.*

2. **Benthic grab** *This apparatus gouges out and grabs a chunk of the seafloor. The sample reveals what kinds of small animals, such as worms and tiny shrimplike amphipods, live on and in the bottom of the ocean.*

3. **Guyots** *An undersea volcano or an eroded volcanic island is called a seamount. Guyots are flat-topped seamounts. They once had tips near or above the sea surface, but wave action eroded the tips away. Most guyots are found in the Pacific Ocean.*

4. **Subduction zone** *At a subduction zone, one crustal plate slides under another, creating a trench.*

5. **Remotely operated vehicles** *Remotely operated vehicles, called ROVs, are equipped with cameras and other instruments. They can provide sharp images of marine animals, seafloor features, and other underwater objects, such as sunken ships.*

6. **Ocean trench** *An ocean trench is a long, deep split in the seafloor where an ocean plate is sliding under another plate. The Mariana Trench in the western Pacific Ocean is Earth's deepest trench. It plunges more than 36,100 feet (11,022 m) and is deeper than Hawaii is high.*

How do we know what is down below?

Many types of special instruments, such as underwater cameras, sonar devices that track sound waves, and other tools, help scientists to learn about the world hidden beneath the waves.

Under the sea
Deep ocean basins are where trenches, ridges of undersea mountains, and flat abyssal plains are found. They make up more than half of Earth's surface.

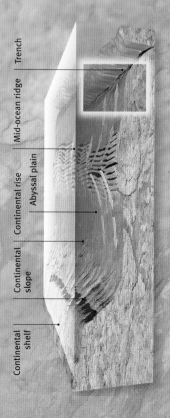

Continental shelf | Continental slope | Continental rise | Abyssal plain | Mid-ocean ridge | Trench

The Ocean
In Motion

Waves and tides are two of the ocean's most striking features, and oceanographers spent many years working to understand what causes them. An ocean wave develops when energy from an outside force sets seawater in motion, sometimes over thousands of miles. Most waves are wind waves, so named because wind energy creates them. Another type of wave, called a seismic wave or tsunami, develops when an undersea earthquake, landslide, or volcanic eruption jolts the ocean floor. Ocean tides are vast, shallow waves, and the only ones that are predictable. They are caused by the pull of gravity.

Break point *As a wave makes its way closer to shore, friction slows the base of the wave and the wave crest breaks over it.*

Inside a wave *Water particles inside a wave circle up, forward, down, and back.*

Ocean currents
Wind energy helps to create ocean currents. Some of these streams of moving water travel in huge loops called gyres. As this map shows, there is a gyre in each of the five largest ocean areas. Cool currents are shown in blue and warm currents are shown in red.

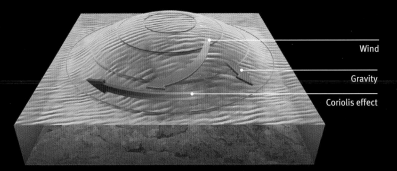

Wind

Gravity

Coriolis effect

Shifting currents
Gravity pulls ocean currents toward low pressure areas. Earth's rotation also deflects currents clockwise (to the right) in the Northern Hemisphere and counterclockwise (to the left) in the Southern Hemisphere. This shift is called the Coriolis effect.

How is a wave measured?
A wind wave curves up to a narrow crest, then curls down to a hollow called a trough. The distance between the crests of two waves is the wavelength. The height of a wave is the distance between a wave crest and the troughs on either side of it.

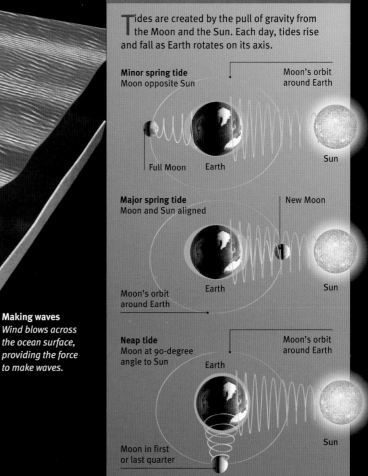

IRRESISTIBLE FORCE

Tides are created by the pull of gravity from the Moon and the Sun. Each day, tides rise and fall as Earth rotates on its axis.

Minor spring tide
Moon opposite Sun

Moon's orbit around Earth

Full Moon   Earth   Sun

Major spring tide
Moon and Sun aligned

New Moon

Moon's orbit around Earth

Earth   Sun

Neap tide
Moon at 90-degree angle to Sun

Moon's orbit around Earth

Earth

Moon in first or last quarter

Sun

Making waves
Wind blows across the ocean surface, providing the force to make waves.

Crest

Trough

Coming in to land
As waves approach land, wave crests become sharper and the wavelength is shorter.

Hitting the brakes
Waves slow down as they reach the shallows because friction with the ocean bottom acts like a brake.

Tsunami

A tsunami (pronounced soo NAH mee) grows higher as it nears land. The rushing wall of water can travel faster than 470 miles per hour (756 k/h), and 100-foot (30-m) waves, the height of a 10-story building, can slam ashore. In 2004 a tsunami destroyed the entire city of Banda Aceh, Indonesia (right).

Oceans and
Climate

Just as wind blowing over the ocean creates waves, other air–sea interactions help shape both weather and climate. Sunny skies, rain, and storms are examples of weather–the day-to-day conditions in a particular place. A region's climate is the long-term pattern of these conditions. Huge masses of air that move high above Earth carry a great deal of water in gas form, called water vapor. Much of this vapor is made up of water that has evaporated from the ocean. Water vapor in the atmosphere may travel thousands of miles before it falls back to Earth as rain or snow. When strong winds pick up the falling water, the stage is set for a raging storm.

MOVING ON UP

Upwelling is a process that regularly brings deep, cold ocean water up toward the surface. Like a conveyor belt, this rising cold water carries sunken bits of food back to shallower areas, where it nourishes fish and other sea creatures. When upwelling is interrupted, marine life may starve.

Where the fish are
Fishing fleets deploy their gear in areas where large numbers of fish swim near the surface.

Warm coastal water
Warm surface water moves offshore and is replaced by cold water upwelling from below.

Wind-driven currents
Winds blowing along the coast create an ocean current that moves warm coastal water offshore.

A fish food bonanza An ample supply of food supports large populations of fish in places where upwelling occurs.

Upwelling water
Cold upwelling water is rich in substances that plankton feed on.

The El Niño effect
When an unusual warm current called El Niño (the Christ child) flows across the Pacific toward South America, it prevents upwelling there. Food for marine life vanishes, and the weather changes in these regions.

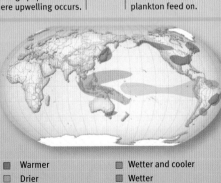

- ▢ Warmer
- ▢ Drier
- ▢ Wetter and warmer
- ▢ Wetter and cooler
- ▢ Wetter

Global climate change
Human activities, such as burning gasoline, put huge amounts of carbon dioxide and other gases into Earth's atmosphere. The gases build up and act like a blanket that is warming the atmosphere. As a result, in many regions of Earth, the climate is changing.

Melting ice
The ocean is warming and ice at the poles is melting. This photograph shows sea ice breaking up near Antarctica.

A superstorm
A hurricane can become enormous—more than 620 miles (1,000 km) across and nearly 10 miles (16 km) high.

What is a cloud? *A cloud is a mass of droplets of water vapor. Storm clouds appear dark from land because they hold a great deal of water vapor.*

The birth of a hurricane

Storms form when warm ocean water evaporates upward and the air begins moving in a counter-clockwise circle. A hurricane is a spinning mass of warm, moist air that occurs when winds reach a speed of 74 miles per hour (118 km/h). The word "hurricane" comes from "Huracan," a Caribbean Indian name for the "God of the Wind." Elsewhere hurricanes are called cyclones or typhoons.

Flooding
Earth's sea level is rising as meltwater flows into the ocean. In the future, flooding along seacoasts will occur more often.

More storms
A warming ocean will probably fuel more tropical storms, including hurricanes. This picture shows a storm lashing a California beach house.

Coral bleaching
Warming seas are a factor in coral bleaching, which often kills the coral polyps. These bleached corals are in Australia's Great Barrier Reef.

An upward spiral *Spiraling winds carry warm, wet air upward, where it cools. Water vapor condenses into droplets that fall as torrential rain. It often takes several days for a full-blown hurricane to develop.*

Whirling bands of rain clouds *As the storm builds, spiraling bands of rain clouds form. The outer bands may be more than 200 miles (320 km) from the center of the hurricane.*

Devastation *Hurricane winds have been clocked at 250 miles per hour (400 km/h). A large hurricane can dump 20 billion tons (18 billion t) of rainwater in a day—causing terrible damage on shore.*

Eye of the storm *The center, or "eye," of a hurricane is eerily calm compared to the wind-whipped rainbands. The eye is usually about 8 to 10 miles (13 to 16 km) across.*

Regions and Zones
Ocean Habitats

The ocean is much more than crashing waves, powerful currents, and changing tides. It is a place every bit as rich in life as the land. Water depth, temperature, and the amount of sunlight all help to determine the number of organisms and species in different parts of the ocean realm. The ocean is divided into three layers: a narrow upper band of sunlit water, a dim middle layer, and the inky black depths below. The majority of marine creatures live in or on the seafloor, a narrow zone that stretches all the way from the shore to the bottom of the deepest ocean trench. Other species live in open water and rarely, if ever, visit the seafloor. Scientists estimate that there are at least half a million different species of marine life.

Watery regions
The warmest ocean water is in the tropics; the coldest is in polar seas. The surface water temperature in temperate regions falls between these two extremes. The temperature of seawater affects what kind of creatures live in each region.

Tropical regions ▪ Temperate regions ▪ Polar regions

From top to bottom: ocean zones
Ocean waters are divided into three main zones according to the amount of sunlight that reaches them. Scientists also divide the seafloor into zones according to their different depths.

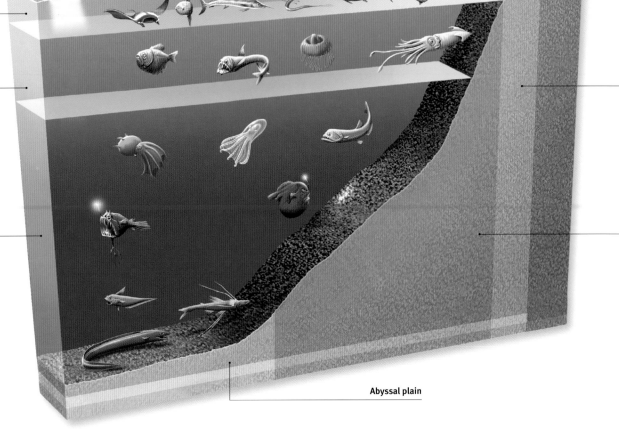

Sunlight zone
Surface down to
660 feet (200 m)

Twilight zone
660 down to
3,300 feet
(200–1,000 m)

Dark zone
3,300 feet
(1,000 m) all the
way to bottom

Shore

Continental shelf

Continental slope

Abyssal plain

Warm surface, cold depths

Heat from the sun warms the upper layer of the ocean, where most marine organisms live. Although the polar seas are icy and tropical waters are warm, below the sunlight zone—about 660 feet (200 m)—the ocean is cold all around the globe.

Polar life *Few animal species live year-round in polar seas. Some polar fish have blood that does not freeze. Walruses, whales, and polar bears have insulating fat or fur to stay warm.*

Temperate life *Many animals migrate through the ocean's temperate waters as the seasons change. Most of the fish that humans eat are caught in temperate seas.*

Tropical life *The water and seafloor in warm tropical regions contain the greatest diversity of marine species. Coral reefs, which are sometimes called rain forests of the sea, form in these regions where the bottom is rocky.*

Warm tropical waters
The surface temperature of tropical seas is usually warmer than 69°F (20°C). In some areas, shallow waters may be a warm, bathlike 85°F (29°C).

Icy polar seas
The average surface temperature of polar seas is below 45°F (5°C). In winter when sea ice forms, the temperature of polar seas is much colder.

Hot and cold *In temperate regions, the ocean's surface averages a cool 50°F (10°C), but seas may be warmer in summer and colder in winter.*

Made for the Ocean
Adaptations

Many ocean species have special body features that help them survive in their habitats and produce young. These features are called adaptations. For example, fish have gills that take up oxygen from the water; air-breathing marine animals, such as whales, seals, and sea turtles, can hold their breath underwater for long periods while they dive; and fast-swimming predators, such as mako sharks, have sleek bodies and sharp teeth for piercing and holding prey. Many adaptations are for defense. These lifesaving adaptations include the prickly spines of a sea urchin, poisonous venom, and a clam's ability to burrow into sand or mud on the bottom. Still other sea creatures are masters of camouflage—their body shape or color pattern is adapted to blend in with their surroundings.

Strong swimming muscles *A tuna needs sturdy muscles for its lifetime of swimming. Muscle is the "meat" of a fish. One of the reasons that bluefin tunas are endangered is because so many people prize their flesh as food.*

A natural keel *A curving keel-like structure at the base of a tuna's tail is another special drag-reducing adaptation.*

Crescent-shaped tail
The bluefin has a narrow, stiff tail fin shaped like a crescent moon. This shape reduces turbulence or "drag" that can slow the tuna's movement through the water.

Finlets *Small, pointed, movable finlets smooth out the flow of water over the tuna's tail.*

Warm muscles *A network of blood vessels called a* rete mirabile, *or "wonderful net," keeps warm blood flowing to a tuna's muscles. This allows tunas to swim faster as they hunt for food in cold ocean waters.*

GETTING IN THE SWIM
Swimmers of the past

Fish have been swimming in the sea for more than 440 million years. But they are not the only creatures to cruise the ocean. Other animals, such as reptiles and mammals, also evolved adaptations for efficient swimming.

Fishlike ichthyosaurs Ichthyosaurs were ancient marine reptiles shaped like fish. They could swim an estimated 25 miles per hour (40 km/h), but went extinct about 90 million years ago.

Paddling plesiosaurs Plesiosaurs had large paddle-like flippers. Fossils of these ancient swimming reptiles show that some plesiosaurs were up to 46 feet (14 m) long, equal to about eight men lying end to end. Plesiosaurs went extinct at the same time as the dinosaurs, about 65 million years ago.

Swimming torpedo *The bluefin's body is roughly shaped like a torpedo. This streamlining helps save energy, so the tuna can swim faster with less effort.*

Folding fins *For extra streamlining, the dorsal fin of a bluefin folds down when the tuna is swimming very fast, such as when it chases prey. The pectoral fins also fold up and back into a groove on the bluefin's side.*

Oxygen from gills *The bright red gills of a bluefin are pleated like an air filter. Together the folds have a large surface area to supply plenty of oxygen as the tuna swims.*

A predator's large eyes *Large eyes help tunas spot prey both close to the surface and in deeper waters.*

Countershading *The back of a bluefin tuna is dark blue, but its bottom and sides are silvery. This countershading makes it harder for both predators and prey to see a bluefin in the water.*

Swim or die *To keep oxygen-rich water flowing over its gills, a bluefin must swim constantly with its mouth open throughout its life, never stopping to rest. Constant swimming also keeps bluefins from sinking.*

A rigid body *As a bluefin swims, it holds its body quite stiff. This behavior is another way of keeping drag and turbulence low.*

Leafy sea dragon

The yellow-green color and frilly leaflike appendages of a leafy sea dragon camouflage it in the seaweed beds where it lives. This odd fish uses its pointy snout to suck up small shrimplike prey. Unlike the fast-swimming bluefin, a sea dragon is adapted to hang around the seabed and nip prey from stationary seaweed.

Built for speed: the bluefin tuna

From its bullet-like body to its crescent-shaped tail, a bluefin tuna's adaptations make it a powerful high-seas predator. Its cruising speed is about two miles per hour (1.3 km/h), fast for a fish. When chasing prey, however, a tuna can accelerate in a burst of speed, reaching 12 to 18 miles per hour (20–30 km/h) in less than 10 seconds.

Swimmers of the present

The mighty mako Mako sharks have many of the same adaptations for efficient swimming, such as streamlining and countershading, that we see in tunas. When two unrelated animals evolve similar adaptations, it is called convergence.

Mammals of the sea Dolphins are mammals that evolved adaptations for life in the sea, such as their fishlike body shape and sophisticated use of sound for underwater communication. However, they still breathe air, as do whales, seals, sea lions, and sea otters.

Great Ocean
Migrations

Some creatures of the sea make vast journeys across the oceans. These long-distance travelers include birds and whales, sea turtles, and several kinds of sharks. Using cues from the sun, sounds, odors, or even Earth's magnetic field, migrators can find their way to destinations thousands of miles from their starting point. When the time is right, they then retrace their path. Sometimes the journey's goal is finding a mate or a location that provides food and shelter for the young. Where temperature and other ocean conditions change with the seasons, the ability to migrate also can mean the difference between life and death.

Tracking loggerhead sea turtles
Scientists use satellites to study the migration of loggerhead sea turtles. Loggerheads swim thousands of miles through the Atlantic Ocean. They navigate by sensing changes in Earth's magnetic field.

Turtle transmitter Scientists glue a satellite transmitter on to the turtle's shell.

Satellite signals Signals from the transmitter beam up to a satellite when the turtle swims at the surface.

Tracking station The satellite beams the information down to a tracking station.

Computer records A computer receives the signal and records the turtle's location.

Scientific research Scientists monitor the turtle's path and use this information in their research.

Arctic tern Arctic terns migrate from arctic North America, across the Atlantic, all the way to Antarctica—a trip of more than 12,000 miles (19,000 km).

Gray whale Gray whales migrate farther than any other mammal on Earth. They summer in the north Pacific but spend winter 5,000 miles (8,000 km) south, off Baja California, Mexico, where they mate.

Blue shark Blue sharks migrate across the Atlantic and back each year, hitchhiking on the looping ocean current called the Gulf Stream.

Dangerous moves
Ocean migrations are long and uncertain voyages. Many migrating animals will not survive storms, predators, or other natural threats. Fishing fleets rely on knowledge of migration routes to find the best places to catch migrating fish.

Adult loggerhead *It takes at least 20 years for a loggerhead to grow into an adult. Only a few hatchlings survive this long.*

TO THE SEA AND BACK

Male loggerheads spend their whole lives in the ocean. After mating, females migrate to the same beach where they hatched many years before.

1 First encounter
Adult males and females meet in the Atlantic Ocean.

2 Mysterious mating
Loggerheads mate at sea. Scientists know little about this mysterious event.

3 Laying eggs
The female returns to her native beach and lays her eggs in the sand.

4 Hatchlings
Hatched baby turtles scurry to the surf and begin their ocean journey.

5 Growing up After growing for many years, adult turtles will be ready to mate.

Young loggerhead *Tucked in a tangle of green-brown seaweed, a young loggerhead has a better chance of avoiding predators.*

Life in the Sargasso Sea
Baby loggerheads navigate into the Gulf Stream. This strong current carries them to an area called the Sargasso Sea, where huge mats of seaweed float at the ocean surface. Here the young turtles live and grow, probably for several years.

Oceans Under
Threat

Vast as it seems, the ocean is in danger. With nearly 7 billion humans on our planet, more and more people are living along coasts and there are ever more mouths to feed. A major problem is overfishing—too many boats taking too many fish, day after day. At the same time, oil spills, sewage, runoff from farmland, dumping from ships, and chemicals from industries are polluting the seas. Homes, towns, and cities are replacing natural shores. The more we understand these threats, the more citizens and governments can take steps to protect the ocean and the creatures that call it home.

World Heritage sites

Coastal nations around the world have created more than two dozen undersea World Heritage sites (shown by red dots). These sites, and their treasures, are recognized internationally as areas worth protecting for future generations. They include historical shipwrecks and beautiful coral reefs. Divers and snorkelers can visit many of these special places.

THREATENED SPECIES

Different kinds of human activities put marine species in danger. Unless we take steps to protect them, many sea creatures may go extinct.

Blue whales Blue whales are Earth's largest animals. Due to whaling, only a few remain.

Leatherback sea turtles All sea turtles are endangered, partly because people in some areas eat turtle eggs and meat, or kill them for their shells.

Albatrosses These large seabirds are often caught by fishing nets and hooks as they look for food.

Sand tiger sharks Overfishing is a major threat to these sharks.

Mangroves People destroy mangrove forests to make space for activities such as shrimp farming.

Corals Polluted water is killing corals in some areas. Reefs are destroyed by people fishing with explosives.

Creating an artificial reef

Around the world, old ships, such as this one, are deliberately sunk to create artificial reefs on the seafloor. They provide homes for many forms of ocean life. For example, sea anemones and some mollusks live only where they can attach to a hard surface, and some fish only where they can hide.

Ready to sink After this old ship has been cleaned and any hazardous material is removed, it is sunk in a specific place to form an artificial reef.

Colonization In a few months, anemones and other life forms begin to make the wreck their new home. The sunken wreck also protects the seabed.

Seafloor oasis With time, a community of species form an oasis of life on the seafloor. Both the number and diversity of animals in and around the artificial reef will continue to increase with time.

Overfishing to extinction

Modern fishing boats catch tons of fish in a single haul of the net. Some species, such as cod and bluefin tuna, have been seriously overfished and are now under threat.

Oil spill emergency

Oil spills are major ocean disasters. A famous spill occurred in 1989 when the supertanker *Exxon Valdez* went aground in Prince William Sound, in Alaska, USA. Only about 22 percent of the ship's cargo of oil leaked out of its damaged hull, but efforts to clean it up took years and cost billions of dollars.

1   **Exxon Valdez** *The Exxon Valdez runs aground. About 11 million gallons (40 million l) of crude oil leaks out into the ocean.*

2   **Helicopter spray** *A helicopter sprays a strong detergent. The spray only helps disperse about five percent of the oil.*

3   **Shore rocks and sand** *Oily shore rocks and sand are rinsed with*

very hot water. Scientists later learn that the hot water killed many small shore animals. It will take years for the shore to recover.

4   **Oil slick** *About one-third of the oil forms a shiny slick on the water. Oil also washes up along at least 400 miles (600 km) of the Alaskan coastline.*

5   **Workforce** *More than 11,000 workers help clean up the spill.*

6   **Containment booms** *Containment booms enclose large areas of oil above and below the surface. A small amount of oil is burned off. Some is pumped out by a skimmer ship. Much of the oil evaporates.*

7   **Marine life** *Oil-soaked birds are cleaned with absorbent pads. Some survive but hundreds of thousands die. Sea otters, whales, and millions of fish and fish eggs also die.*

Deep-sea
Legends

The ocean depths have always inspired people to wonder what might lurk below the surface. Long before scientists had the tools to explore the deep, sea lore was full of stories of fearsome monsters and mysterious mermaids. Some of these myths and legends were fanciful tales, but others may have been based on real events. An example is Kraken, a giant octopus-like creature that was said to attack ships at sea. Some believe that the legend of Kraken grew from the stories of fishermen who were amazed to see giant squid, which have long tentacles and may grow to more than 20 feet (6 m).

Attack of the sea serpent

Early mariners were at the mercy of storms and other mishaps. Many believed that huge snakelike sea serpents could attack unlucky vessels. A real sea creature that might have been mistaken for a sea serpent is the oarfish. This eel-like fish has sharp red spikes running down its back and may be 25 feet (7.6 m) long.

Women of the waves
Stories of mermaids, with long flowing hair and fish tails, come from many seafaring peoples. Mermaids called sirens were blamed for singing songs that lured ships to wreck on rocky shores.

Krakens
Fishermen from Norway may have been the first to mention krakens. Huge and horrible, krakens supposedly could wrap their tentacles around a sailing ship and pull it under the waves.

Lost city
Legend says that an island city called Atlantis was washed into the sea after a massive earthquake. One theory is that Atlantis was a real city on, or near, the Greek island of Crete in the Mediterranean Sea.

Highways for
Exploration

For thousands of years, mariners traveled the seas in search of new lands, riches, and adventure. Ancient Egyptians, Polynesians, and Vikings were some of the first ocean explorers. In the beginning there were no maps or charts: seafarers had to navigate using the stars and their knowledge of currents and winds. Long voyages could take months or years. Storms, disease, and other dangers lurked in the ocean expanses. Countless expeditions left port and were never seen again. Over the centuries, mariners developed a tool kit of instruments to help them explore the seas—and with luck, return safely home again.

To the edge of Earth
Many early peoples believed that Earth was flat. Some feared that ships could sail right off the edge of Earth and into the clutches of a dragon if they ventured too far from the shore.

Ships to reach new lands

For most of history, ocean travel was driven only by human muscle power and the wind. Builders used ingenuity and experience to develop seaworthy vessels. By 1876 Earth's land masses had all been discovered, and explorers changed their focus to uncover secrets of the deep.

1 **4000–3000 BC: Ancient Egyptian trading boats**
Ancient Egyptians used bundled papyrus reeds to make the hull and other parts of their boats. These vessels usually stayed within sight of land.

2 **1500 BC–AD 300: Polynesian canoes cross the Pacific**
Polynesians were experts at reading currents and winds for journeys across the South Pacific. Their outrigger canoes were up to 100 feet (30 m) long.

6 **1492: The *Santa Maria*: flagship of Columbus** *The* Santa Maria, *a bulky cargo ship, was the main ship in Columbus's fleet during his voyage across the Atlantic, from Spain to North America, in 1492. The ill-fated ship went aground on Christmas Day in Haiti, 1492.*

7 **1519–1552: Magellan's *Victoria*** *The* Victoria *was the first ship to sail around the world. Its Portuguese captain Magellan was killed in 1521 during the voyage but his crew sailed on. Of the five vessels and 285 crew that began the journey, only the Victoria and a handful of sailors made it home again.*

HOW DID SAILORS KNOW WHERE TO GO?

Mariners of old navigated by the Sun and stars. Early instruments measured latitude, a ship's location north or south of the equator. Later inventions measured longitude, a ship's location east or west of a starting point.

Cross staff

A cross staff was more accurate than an astrolabe. Both forced the user to look in two places—at the horizon and at the Sun or Polaris—and were useless in cloudy weather.

Astrolabe

Early mariners used an astrolabe to find a ship's latitude. Its dial and arms roughly measured the ship's position relative to the Sun or to Polaris, the North Star.

Sextant

In a sextant, small mirrors reflect the Sun's image. Now a navigator could view the sun's position and the horizon together.

Chronometer

A marine chronometer is a precise clock that keeps the time of a fixed location. By comparing local time with the chronometer, a navigator can calculate a ship's longitude.

5 **1400–1500: Portuguese explorers**
Caravels were three-masted ships first used by Portuguese explorers in the 1400s searching for trade routes to India. These ships were small and easy to maneuver.

3 **300 BC–AD 200: Chinese pioneers**
Chinese mariners pioneered the "junk"—the first ship with more than one mast. They also invented the rudder and compass. Junks are still used in modern China.

4 **AD 700–1000: Viking warriors**
Vikings explored the North Atlantic in sleek ships powered by oars and a sail. They reached North America more than 1,000 years ago, long before Columbus arrived.

8 **1768–1771: Captain Cook and the HMS *Endeavour***
The English captain Cook commanded the Endeavour *on an expedition to Tahiti. During the voyage he also explored New Zealand and the east coast of Australia. Before its voyage of discovery, the* Endeavour *was a collier—a vessel used to haul coal.*

9 **1872–1876: HMS *Challenger***
The Challenger *was the first ship used to study the deep sea. From this time onward, attention shifted from exploring the surface to exploring the deep. Scientists on board discovered the Mariana Trench, the deepest place in the ocean.*

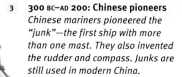

Standing rigging *Not all parts of the rigging were used to move sails. Thick ropes called shrouds helped hold a galleon's masts in place. Sailors climbed up rope ladders to make repairs or scan the horizon.*

The *Golden Hind*

A famous small galleon, the *Golden Hind*, captained by the English adventurer Sir Francis Drake, might have looked like this. The ship was 20 feet (6 m) wide and 70 feet (21 m) long, equal to about 12 men lying end to end. It carried 16 cannon.

Sails *Sail makers sewed sails from heavy canvas cloth that could withstand wind, rain, and sun. Sails were hung from long spars, or "yards," made from pine trees.*

Bowsprit *The bowsprit supported lines used to help change the position of the sails on the foremast. The beaklike projection beneath it was called the ram.*

Jib *A sail deployed in front of the bow was called a jib.*

Inside and Out
Galleon

Galleons were among the most important sail-powered ships of all time. Beginning in the 1500s, seafaring nations such as Spain and England used galleons for trade, sea battles, and exploration of far-off lands. A galleon was a complicated ship, with several decks, cannon and other guns, and three or more masts to support its sails. Large galleons could carry hundreds of sailors and passengers plus cargo and food for several months. The shipwrights who built galleons did not have written plans. Instead they used a method called rack-of-eye—a mental image of how various parts should fit together. Even with an experienced work crew, it usually took two years to complete the ship.

Below decks *The interior of a galleon was used mainly for storage. Sailors might sleep surrounded by bags of rice, barrels of salted meat, and crates of hard crackers called hard tack. Some ships carried chickens and cows to provide eggs, milk, and fresh meat. There was little good drinking water.*

Keel *The keel is a ship's backbone that runs from the front, or bow, to the rear, or stern. For galleons, it was usually made of a hard, durable wood, such as oak or mahogany.*

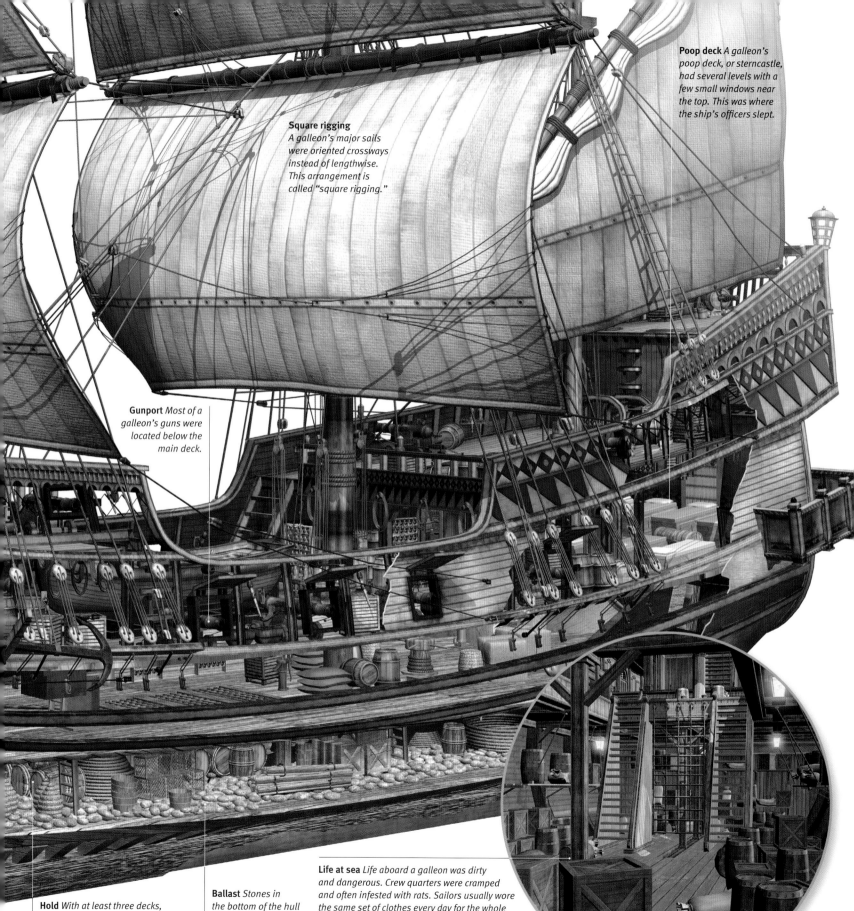

Poop deck *A galleon's poop deck, or sterncastle, had several levels with a few small windows near the top. This was where the ship's officers slept.*

Square rigging
A galleon's major sails were oriented crossways instead of lengthwise. This arrangement is called "square rigging."

Gunport *Most of a galleon's guns were located below the main deck.*

Hold *With at least three decks, even small galleons could carry 500 tons (454 t) of cargo. The hold also stored spare rigging for repairs.*

Ballast *Stones in the bottom of the hull added ballast—weight that helped keep the ship from tipping over.*

Life at sea *Life aboard a galleon was dirty and dangerous. Crew quarters were cramped and often infested with rats. Sailors usually wore the same set of clothes every day for the whole voyage, which could last for months. Everyone used the same filthy toilet. Many sailors died of disease or injuries before their vessel returned home.*

The Ocean's Hidden
Dangers

Going to sea has always been a risky proposition. From the beginning, seafarers faced raging storms that could capsize ships or blow them far off course. In many places pirates lurked, ready to plunder ships and kill their crews. Other perils were close to shore. Before mariners had advanced navigation instruments, ships and boats were often wrecked on rocky shores or went aground in hidden shallows. Today's oceangoing ships have sophisticated technology that makes voyages much safer. Still, in many ocean regions, seafarers must be on the alert for modern-day pirates, hurricanes, and other dangers that lurk just beyond the horizon.

Dangerous waters *Before ships had electronic navigation aids, fog and storms made sailing close to shore risky. Lighthouses and buoys were built to help guide ships into port.*

Pirate perils

Pirates were one of the most feared dangers of ocean voyages. Sometimes several pirate ships would band together and form a pirate armada—a fleet of fearless maritime thieves. Sometimes they also raided towns in search of gold, silver, and other treasure.

Death on the rocks *When a ship crashed onto rocks, wreckers hiding on shore made their surprise attack. The ship's crew were often murdered, or drowned as they tried to escape.*

A TITANIC DISASTER

The RMS *Titanic* was a marvel of technology and people believed it was unsinkable. But during its first voyage, on April 14, 1912, an iceberg in the North Atlantic tore open *Titanic*'s hull. The huge ship sank in less than three hours. More than 1,500 passengers and crew perished in the icy water.

Call for help As *Titanic* began to sink, the crew sent a wireless SOS. It was the first time in history that a ship at sea used this international distress signal.

Not enough boats The ship had 20 lifeboats—not nearly enough to hold all of its 2,200 passengers and crew. Only 705 people survived the disaster.

Signal fires *Before lighthouses, signal fires on shore marked dangerous rocks or hidden sandbars. Pirate bands, called wreckers, lured ships to their doom by moving the fires so that ships were unaware of hazardous passages.*

Buccaneers *Pirates of old were also called buccaneers. Both men and women took up this ruthless profession. Some pirates became privateers—they offered their services to government officials. In return privateers were allowed to attack ships belonging to the government's enemies.*

Exploring the
Depths

The ocean covers 75 percent of Earth's surface, yet for humans it is a dangerous place. Drowning is the first risk: human lungs cannot get oxygen from water, as fish do. Another problem is pressure. Below about 50 feet (15 m), water pressure begins to strain the lungs and other tissues, and this danger grows sharply as the depth increases. However, humans have not let these challenges stop them from learning about the seas. Instead, generations of scientists and inventors have harnessed technology to probe ever deeper into the ocean. From diving suits and SCUBA gear to navy submarines and research submersibles, humans have devised ways to work, study, and explore the undersea world.

Pioneers under the sea

Inventors and engineers have tried different approaches for underwater vehicles. Submarines are designed to operate in shallow water, but submersibles are made to explore the deep ocean. They must be strong enough to withstand the great pressure of the ocean's depths.

Holland submarine J. P. Holland built the first modern submarine (below) in 1900. It had a gasoline engine, a torpedo tube, and batteries to propel it underwater.

The *Turtle* In 1775 D. Bushnell built the *Turtle* submarine (above) to attack British warships during the American Revolution. It was made from wood and sank the first time it was used.

Trieste The bathyscaphe *Trieste* was the first crew-controlled submersible. In 1960, with a two-man crew, it descended 35,800 feet (10,900 m). This is the deepest dive on record.

Shinkai 6500 This Japanese submersible is the deepest diver in current use, descending a maximum of 21,300 feet (6,500 m). It can carry three people and stay submerged for eight hours, allowing scientists to collect samples and take photographs of the deep.

Aquarius undersea laboratory

Aquarius is an undersea laboratory dedicated to marine science. Here, scientists have the time to set up complicated experiments and obtain results that would take much longer to achieve if they had to keep surfacing. Aquarius is located about three miles (4.5 km) off Key Largo, Florida, USA. Air and power is supplied to the laboratory by a life-support buoy floating on the ocean's surface.

Sleeping area *Aquarius has a crew of six scientists, called aquanauts. They sleep here in bunkbeds.*

Kitchen and work area *The kitchen has a sink, refrigerator, microwave, and hot water dispenser. The work area has computer stations.*

Window to another world *Aquanauts can look out two large round windows called viewports.*

Support legs *For stability, each of the four support legs contains 25 tons (23 t) of lead. The legs are adjustable to keep the structure level.*

DIVING INTO THE DEEP

Since the early 1800s diving technology has evolved to allow divers to stay underwater longer, and dive deeper and deeper.

1829: diving helmet Brothers C. and J. Deane develop a diving helmet with air supplied by a tube from the surface.

1865: air from a tank B. Rouquayrol and A. Denayrouze develop a tethered breathing system that uses a tank of compressed air.

1876: compressed oxygen H. Fluess invents a diving suit with a built-in oxygen supply.

1919: diver control of air Ohgushi's Peerless Respirator allows divers to breathe through their noses and switch air on and off.

1940: Aqua-Lung J. Cousteau and E. Gagnan develop the Aqua-Lung. Oxygen flows from a self-contained tank as a diver breathes.

1970s: JIM Inventors develop a one-person submersible fitted to the body. Today's latest models are used by the US Navy for dives as deep down as 2,000 feet (600 m).

Aquanauts *Aquarius scientists leave the surface world on missions that last up to 10 days at a time. They stay underwater, either inside the laboratory or outside on dives. When a mission ends, aquanauts must undergo 17 hours of decompression before it is safe for them to return to the surface.*

Entry lock *This area contains the toilet, worktables for experiments, computers, and small viewports.*

Wet porch *This is a staging area where aquanauts prepare for dives. They are also picked up from here when a mission ends.*

Safe escape *If problems develop inside Aquarius, the crew can escape to this small structure, called a gazebo. It has its own oxygen supply.*

How low does it go? *Aquarius is submerged about 66 feet (20 m) below the surface, next to a coral reef. The laboratory is about 46 feet (14 m) long and 9 feet (3 m) wide.*

The Ocean's
Bounty

From the sea surface to the deep abyss, the oceans are a treasure trove of valuable products and substances. Seafood, oil, natural gas, and even potential medicines are on the list. Fisheries harvest millions of tons of wild fish and shellfish each year. More and more oil rigs are sprouting up along seacoasts, and exploration of the seafloor has located large pools of natural gas. In places, deposits of important minerals, including manganese, nickel, and gold, lie on the bottom. Scientists are working on methods to gather these minerals without harming the undersea environment. People also are looking for ways to harness the ocean's wind and wave energy for use in homes and industry.

Derrick *A derrick supports an oil rig's drilling machinery. Some rigs have dozens of drills. The crude oil is pumped into tankers that carry it to refineries, which produce gasoline and other petroleum products.*

Drilling for black gold

An offshore oil rig houses both the equipment and workers needed to drill for oil. It is like a combination factory and apartment building at sea. Some rigs float while others rest atop pillars sunk into the seafloor. This type of rig may operate for 25 years or more.

Fishing trawler
Each year commercial fishing vessels like this trawler remove billions of tons of seafood from ocean waters. Stocks of some species are being harvested faster than they produce young. As a result overfishing has become a major ecological concern.

Support pillars *The steel or concrete supports for an oil rig must withstand the force of waves and currents. In some areas ice is another threat.*

MARINE MEDICINE AND RESEARCH

Some forms of sea life are allies in the search for new medical drugs or treatments. Scientists are studying others to learn more about how the human body functions.

Sea hare By examining the nerves of a large snail called the sea hare, researchers have learned more about how the human nervous system works.

Sea snails Poisonous cone snails from the Pacific Ocean produce chemicals that scientists are studying for use as powerful painkillers in humans.

Mussel glue Mussels use a natural glue to stay attached to wave-washed rocks. Chemists have used this substance to develop strong adhesives for commercial products.

Helicopter pad *Helicopters ferry workers and supplies to and from the rig, which may be many miles offshore.*

Salt and minerals
Seawater is a major source of table salt (sodium chloride). Magnesium extracted from seawater is used in cosmetics, toothpaste, animal feed, and many industrial processes.

Office and living spaces *An oil rig may have living quarters for as many as 300 people. Workers spend several weeks at a time living and working on the rig.*

Natural gas
Geologists have discovered a huge reservoir of methane, or natural gas, that is trapped in seafloor sediments. Small amounts bubble up naturally, but scientists are trying to figure out how to tap this reservoir to help the growing demand for energy.

Shellfish farming
Shellfish species, such as oysters and mussels, may be raised in shellfish farms where they grow suspended from floating rafts. Many of the world's precious pearls come from farmed oysters.

Wind and wave energy
Scientists are exploring ocean winds, waves, and tides as sources of energy. In many experimental designs, moving air or water turns turbines hooked up to generators that produce electricity.

Photo feature Real-world habitats from around the globe are featured in these photographs.

COASTAL SEAS: THE FACTS

LOCATION EXAMPLES: Around every continent

ANIMALS: Bony fish, such as herrings, anchovies, salmon, sardines, sea bass, drums, flounders, and sea robins; sharks; whales and dolphins; invertebrates, such as jellyfish, squid, octopus, cuttlefish, and zooplankton

PLANTS: Phytoplankton, such as diatoms

MAJOR THREATS: Overfishing and pollution

PHOTO: Dolphins jump off the coast of Roatán, Honduras

Fast facts Facts at your fingertips give essential information on each habitat.

Depth bar This depth bar indicates how deep under the ocean's surface each habitat can be found.

SANDY SHORES: THE FACTS

LOCATION EXAMPLES: Barrier islands, such as the shore along Gulf of Mexico; South African beaches (main illustration)

ANIMALS: Moon snails, tiger beetles, crabs, clams, mussels, sand hoppers, sand prawns, bluebottles, fish, skates and rays, birds, nesting turtles

PLANTS: Turtle grass, railroad vines in foredunes, sea oats on secondary dunes

MAJOR THREATS: Coastal development, shifting sand dunes

PHOTO: Crantock Beach, North Cornwall, UK

Exploring the
Sandy Shore

Sandy beaches are challenging places to survive. The sun is hot, both the water and winds are salty, and waves are constantly pounding the shore. On the surface, sandy shores have few signs of life—sea birds, a scuttling crab, low plants and grasses in the dunes. But dig a little deeper and sandy shores are bustling. Worms, shrimps, clams, and many other creatures hide in burrows just under the surface. Sand hoppers lurk under bits of driftwood, and a host of other tiny animals live tucked into the spaces between sand grains.

Beach zones

A beach has several zones. The subtidal zone beyond the surf is always underwater. Farther up the beach, the intertidal zone is exposed at low tide but underwater at high tide. Above the intertidal zone is the upper beach where sand dunes may form.

Sea level 0 ft (0 m)

30 ft (10 m)

Beach

Low tide mark

Surface wash slides back to next oncoming breaker

Clams *Clams hide in burrows beneath the sand. Some species have a long siphon that pokes up like a drinking straw and filters out food particles carried in by the waves.*

Burrowing clams *Some burrowing clams are huge. They can grow to the size of a man's boot and burrow deeper than 3 feet (1 m) in the sand.*

Amphipods *These tiny animals are relatives of shrimp and lobsters. Some amphipods hunt for food in the shallows, while others, such as sand hoppers, live on the shore.*

Waves advance

Near shore

Surf zone

Subtidal zone

Intertidal zone

Foredunes

Secondary dunes

Maritime forest

Storm drift line

Shore birds *This sand plover uses its beak to probe the sand for worms and other prey. Shore birds also feed on clams and other small animals in the surf zone.*

Ghost crabs *Pale ghost crabs spend their days in burrows, coming out at night to feed. They are scavengers that eat the remains of dead animals.*

Water filters back

DIFFERENT KINDS OF BEACHES

Beaches can consist of rocks, pebbles, mud, or sand. A sand beach is made of gritty particles that are about the size of a pencil point. The different colors of sand depend on where the particles come from.

Gray sand beach of rock particles

Black sand beach of lava particles

White sand beach of coral particles

Sea level 0 ft (0 m)

30 ft (10 m)

ROCKY SHORES: THE FACTS

LOCATION EXAMPLES: **West Coast of North America, Scotland, New England, Canada's Maritime Provinces**

ANIMALS: **Limpets, chitons, sculpins, anemones, blennies, nudibranches, hermit crabs, carnivorous whelk**

PLANTS: **Brown, red, and green algae, such as sea palms**

MAJOR THREATS: **Pollution and oil spills, severe storms and surf action, ecosystem imbalance caused by overfishing**

PHOTO: **Owl's Head Lighthouse, Maine, USA**

Life Along the
Rocky Shore

Rocky shores are home to complex communities of living things. Rocks and their cracks and crevices provide attachment points and hiding places for a variety of invertebrates—animals without backbones—such as mussels, barnacles, crabs, sea snails, and sea stars. To survive on rocky shores, these creatures must be able to withstand pounding waves and dry times when the tide recedes. Some live in the splash zone high up on rocks, while others dwell lower down where seawater moves in and out with the tides. Others, such as fish and sea urchins, are found only underwater, in the shallows of the subtidal zone.

Sea cliff
Pounding waves slowly eat away at the lower part of a rocky sea cliff. This erosion may create caves in the rock.

Sea arch
Over time, the opening of a cave may extend all the way through the tip of the headland. The result is a sea arch.

Sea stack
As waves continue to wash against the sides of the arch, its top may crumble into the sea. This leaves an island-like chunk of rock called a sea stack.

1 **Barnacles** *Barnacles spend most of their lives inside a shell that is attached to rocks. They capture floating food particles.*

2 **Limpets** *These snails use their broad, sticky foot to creep along in search of algae or other food.*

3 **Chitons** *Chitons are marine mollusks. Clamped tightly to rocks, they look like flattened pill bugs. Chitons have lived on Earth for millions of years.*

4 **Blennies** *Because they are small, blennies may live in tide pools, hiding in rock crevices.*

5 **Nudibranches** *These sea snails do not have a shell. They swim around, feeding on soft-bodied animals, such as sponges. Their bright colors warn predators they are poisonous to eat.*

6 **Mussels** *Shiny black mussels attach to rocks and pilings by fibers called byssal threads. A strong natural glue holds the threads in place.*

7 **Sculpins** *Colorful sculpins cruise among seaweeds. Sculpins are one of the few kinds of fish that are found along most northern rocky coasts, even in icy polar regions.*

8 **Anemones** *Although they resemble flowers, sea anemones are animals that use their stinging tentacles to capture prey. If disturbed, they contract and pull their tentacles inward.*

9 **Sea stars** *Common on rocky shores, in tide pools, and sea caves, sea stars have a spiny skin and use their "arms" to move as they hunt down prey, such as mussels and snails.*

10 **Purple sea urchins** *Sea urchins "walk" on the tips of their long spines, which also protect them from predators. They nip pieces of seaweed with their teeth.*

11 **Hermit crabs** *These crabs live inside the discarded shells of marine snails.*

12 **Crabs** *As they scuttle about, crabs use their sharp pincers to scavenge bits of food from the bottom.*

Adapted for surf and sun

Rocky shores are divided into horizontal zones, some much drier and more exposed than others. Most rocky shore animals, except for fish, have adaptations that protect them from wave action and the drying effects of air.

Moving house As they grow, hermit crabs have to find larger shells to move into.

ESTUARIES: THE FACTS

LOCATION EXAMPLES: Chesapeake Bay, USA; Trinity Inlet, Australia

ANIMALS: Juvenile and migrating fish, including sharks; sea turtles; invertebrates; birds, such as herons and egrets

PLANTS: Eelgrass and sea lettuce, cordgrass in temperate estuaries, mangrove trees in tropical estuaries

MAJOR THREATS: Coastal development, pollution, overfishing, wave and wind damage from hurricanes, ice in cold climates, diseases from aquaculture, such as salmon farms

PHOTO: Tropical estuary, the Whitsundays, Australia

Estuaries

An estuary is a bay where salty ocean water mixes with fresh water from rivers and streams. Where the estuary meets the ocean it is nearly as salty as seawater, while at its head the salinity is low. Yet in an estuary nothing stays the same for long. The mix of salty and fresh water changes each day as tides rise and fall. Heavy rains or drought also shift the balance from salty to fresh or vice versa. Summer heat warms the water, then in winter the temperature may suddenly drop. Despite all these ups and downs, estuaries attract an amazing variety of life.

Where the river meets the sea

Most fish and birds migrate into and out of estuaries as the seasons change. Permanent residents are mostly invertebrates, such as crabs, clams, and worms, as well as plants that live along the shore or in the shallows.

Bird life *Terns, seagulls, herons, ducks, and many other kinds of birds dine on animals and plants in estuary waters or marshes that fringe the shore.*

Mud dwellers *Estuaries have a mud bottom that forms as rivers wash in sediments from land. This mud provides a stable home for countless burrowers, including worms, clams, crabs, and snails.*

DIFFERENT KINDS OF ESTUARIES

Geological forces create different kinds of estuaries. Each one is the result of thousands of years of slow changes.

Coastal lagoon
A coastal lagoon forms when sand bars or islands develop close to shore and prevent rivers from emptying freely into the ocean.

Drowned river valley
Some estuaries form when the sea level rises—as when glaciers melt—and floods the mouth of coastal rivers.

Fjord
A fjord is a flooded river valley that has steep, rocky walls cut by glaciers.

Tectonic estuary
A tectonic estuary forms when seawater floods land that is sinking due to the movements of Earth's crustal plates.

Adult barramundi start swimming toward the estuary after heavy summer rains flood their home river.

River

Barramundi lifecycle *The barramundi is an Australian fish that lives mostly in rivers. Once a year, however, adults move into an estuary to breed—the beginning of a new generation.*

Ocean

Females lay millions of eggs in the estuary and males fertilize them. However, other fish eat most of the eggs, so only a few hatch.

Hatchlings that survive the first days of life drift into tidal creeks and swamps.

Grass grazers *Dugongs are marine mammals that graze on submerged grasses in tropical and subtropical estuaries and rivers.*

Estuary

Juvenile barramundi grow rapidly. When they are about 1 foot (30 cm) long, they swim back up into the river.

Predators attack
Crocodiles and bull sharks prowl the warm waters of tropical estuaries. Where the water temperature varies more, other kinds of sharks and even whales may visit, hunting for young prey.

Sea level 0 ft (0 m)

30 ft (10 m)

500 ft (150 m)

COASTAL SEAS: THE FACTS

LOCATION EXAMPLES: Around every continent

ANIMALS: Bony fish, such as herrings, anchovies, salmon, sardines, sea bass, drums, flounders, and sea robins; sharks; whales and dolphins; invertebrates, such as jellyfish, squid, octopus, cuttlefish, and zooplankton

PLANTS: Phytoplankton, such as diatoms

MAJOR THREATS: Overfishing and pollution

PHOTO: Dolphins jump off the coast of Roatán, Honduras

Abundance in the
Coastal Sea

Coastal seas are shallow compared to the open ocean, but they teem with life. This abundance starts close to the sunlit surface, where tiny floating plants and animals called plankton thrive. Shrimps and small fish that eat plankton become meals for larger predators, such as humpback whales, mackerels, and tunas. Topping the predator list are the ocean's premier hunters—sharks. The coastal realm also includes a variety of jellyfish and squid, and crustaceans, such as crabs and shrimps that scuttle across the seafloor. With so many species, coastal seas are popular for commercial fishing. They produce around 90 percent of the seafood eaten by people around the globe.

Manta ray *A manta ray swims using its large triangular fins. It eats plankton swept in by flaps in front of its mouth.*

HOW DO SHARKS HUNT?

Most sharks have razor-sharp teeth, but different species use different methods to hunt and capture prey.

Wobbegong shark

Thresher shark

Great white shark

Squid *A squid can change the color and pattern of its skin to match its surroundings or evade a predator.*

Wobbegongs rest quietly on the seafloor. Their flat body and blotchy skin help disguise them as they lie in wait for prey, such as small fish, crabs, and lobsters.

A thresher shark slaps through schools of fish with its long, curved tail. It then captures fish that have become disoriented by the stunning blow.

Great white sharks hunt marine mammals, such as dolphins and seals. They are stealth hunters that sneak up on prey from below and attack with a sudden lunge.

Jellyfish *Jellyfish have tentacles that fire harpoon-like threads into prey, injecting the victim with a paralyzing toxin.*

Humpback whales *Instead of teeth, humpbacks have stiff, comblike fibers called baleen that filter out plankton and small fish from seawater.*

Schooling fish *Schools, such as these jacks, provide plenty of food for sharks and other fish-eating predators.*

Sharks rule

Most sharks live in coastal seas and pursue prey smaller than they are. A dangerous few, such as great whites, tiger sharks, and bull sharks, hunt large animals and are not afraid to attack people.

Sand tiger shark *The pointed teeth of a sand tiger shark curve backward into its mouth. This makes it more difficult for a struggling prey fish to escape.*

Cuttlefish *Relatives of octopus and squid, cuttlefish swim by squeezing jets of water out through a narrow tube.*

Sea stars *A sea star's mouth is under its body, so it must climb onto its prey, such as clams.*

Crab *Crabs use their large front pincers to grasp food, such as bits of seaweed or flesh from a fish—dead or alive.*

Sea level
o ft (o m)

150 ft (50 m)

CORAL REEFS: THE FACTS

LOCATION EXAMPLES: Great Barrier Reef, Australia; Moorea Island, Tahiti; Belize Reef, Belize; Malé Atoll, Maldives

ANIMALS: Fish, such as groupers, surgeonfish, clownfish, and moray eels; invertebrates, such as giant clams and sea fans; birds, such as black-capped petrels

PLANTS: Coralline algae and sea whip, palms on shore

MAJOR THREATS: Turbidity, often from runoff, that blocks light; coral harvesting; cyanide and blast fishing; pollution

PHOTO: Bora Bora, a fringing reef in French Polynesia

Colors of the
Coral Reef

Corals are among the most unusual animals in the sea. There are thousands of different coral species. Their soft, cup-shaped bodies, called polyps, are only about the size of a grain of rice. Many polyps produce a hard, outer limestone skeleton, and as they grow and die over hundreds or thousands of years, their hard remains form a coral reef. Microscopic algae live in a polyp's tissues. The alga uses a sunlight-powered process called photosynthesis to make most of the polyp's food. If a polyp loses its partner alga, it "bleaches" white, weakens, and dies much sooner than usual. Scientists are studying the causes of bleaching, which can severely damage coral reefs.

1 **Lionfish** *Stripes, spots, and long ruffled fins help disguise a lionfish.*

2 **Barrel sponge** *This pink barrel sponge has a crusty surface.*

3 **Butterfly fish** *Using its pointed mouth, a butterfly fish picks food from coral nooks and crannies.*

4 **Brain coral** *The wavy lines of thousands of polyps form curving ridges in brain coral.*

5 **Spiny pufferfish** *Spines and an inflatable body help this small fish fend off predators.*

6 **Surgeonfish** *A surgeonfish grazes on algae. It uses a sharp spine near its tail for defense.*

7 **Stingray** *A stingray hunts for fish, crabs, and worms. Its tail spine is covered with venom glands.*

8 **Elkhorn coral** *The skeletons of elkhorn coral polyps fuse together in broad shapes.*

9 **Moray eel** *Snakelike moray eels lurk in reef crevices. They have powerful jaws.*

10 **Lace coral** *This soft coral, found in deeper parts of a reef, does not make a limestone skeleton.*

11 **Barracuda** *Razor-toothed barracudas are predators of smaller reef fish.*

12 **Cleaner wrasse** *Cleaner wrasses wriggle over larger fish, nipping off parasites.*

13 **Anemone fish** *These fish live unharmed among the stinging tentacles of sea anemones.*

14 **Tube sponges** *Like all sponges, tube sponges filter food from seawater that enters through millions of tiny channels. The water flows back out an opening at the top.*

15 **Angelfish** *Angelfish are some of the most colorful inhabitants of coral reefs.*

Largest living structure on Earth

Most coral reefs form in warm, shallow waters and are home to a diverse community of corals, sponges, fish, crustaceans, and other species. Coral reefs can grow to be huge. Australia's Great Barrier Reef is 1,250 miles (2,000 km) long and up to 95 miles (150 km) wide. It is the largest structure on Earth built by living things.

HOW DOES A CORAL ATOLL FORM?

Many coral reefs form around volcanic islands. Over long spans of time, the form of the reef changes as the island sinks back into the ocean.

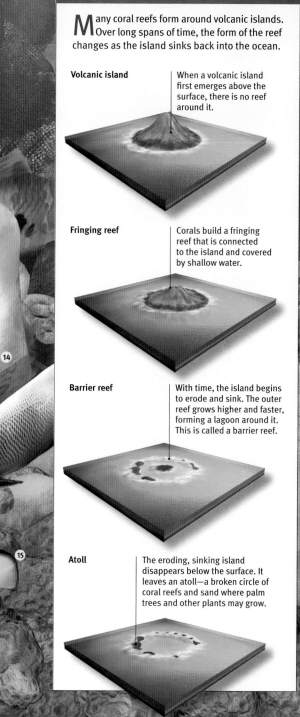

Volcanic island — When a volcanic island first emerges above the surface, there is no reef around it.

Fringing reef — Corals build a fringing reef that is connected to the island and covered by shallow water.

Barrier reef — With time, the island begins to erode and sink. The outer reef grows higher and faster, forming a lagoon around it. This is called a barrier reef.

Atoll — The eroding, sinking island disappears below the surface. It leaves an atoll—a broken circle of coral reefs and sand where palm trees and other plants may grow.

Sea level
0 ft (0 m)

75 ft (25 m)

150 ft (50 m)

KELP FORESTS: THE FACTS

LOCATION EXAMPLES: Chile, Norway, New Zealand, California

ANIMALS: Fish, such as greenlings, rockfish, senorita fish, and blacksmith fish; lobsters; crabs; sponges; abalone; nudibranches; sea-squirts; seals; orca whales

PLANTS: Giant kelp, bull kelp, *Laminaria* species, Ecklonia

MAJOR THREATS: Pollution, increasing seawater temperature, overharvesting of kelps for human food, overharvesting of species, such as sea otters, that eat kelp predators

PHOTO: Underwater forest of kelp, California, USA

Floaters *Pouches filled with gas act like life preservers that help kelp blades float near the surface, where sunlight can reach them.*

Hide-and-Seek in the

Kelp Forest

Towering seaweeds called kelps form lush underwater forests in the shallows along some rocky coasts. Here the water often is calm and the tall kelp stalks sway gently as waves pass by on their way to shore. Kelp forests provide a rich supply of food for sea creatures. Some inhabitants nibble the kelps and other algae, others fill up on the forest's thick soup of drifting plankton. Schools of fish dart by, while sea otters may float at the surface or dive to the bottom for sea urchins. All the while they must be alert for killer whales, which are among the largest predators in the ocean world.

Race to the sun

Kelps need sunlight to survive, so they grow rapidly toward the surface. Some species can grow as fast as 20 inches (50 cm) a day and reach a total height of 130 feet (35 m) or more, higher than a 13-story building.

5

6

WHAT COMES FROM KELP?

Many everyday products contain substances from kelp. Most ice creams, jellies, toothpaste, and soaps contain agar, a thickener that is extracted from kelp.

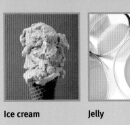

Ice cream   Jelly   Toothpaste

Salad dressing   Glass   Soap

Harvesting kelp
This man is collecting kelp in Ireland.

It's a wrap Japanese chefs use a type of kelp called *honbu* to make sushi rolls.

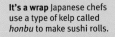

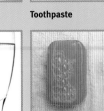

Hanging on *A rootlike holdfast anchors a giant kelp to the rocky bottom.*

1. **Giant kelp** *Giant kelps are extremely sturdy, but a large storm can rip them away from the bottom and destroy an entire kelp forest.*

2. **Sea hare** *Sea hares are large snails that eat algae. Some can weigh as much as 4.5 pounds (10 kg).*

3. **Killer whale** *Killer whales, or orcas, hunt sea otters and fish in the kelp forest.*

4. **Sea otter** *These small marine mammals have thick, soft fur and were almost hunted to extinction.*

5. **California barracudas** *This barracuda species swims in large schools.*

6. **Kelp bass** *Kelp bass are "commuters" that move into and out of the kelp forest as they search for prey.*

7. **Garibaldi** *Bright orange garibaldis tend gardens of algae where they make nests for their young.*

8. **Striped kelpfish** *Living on the seafloor, striped kelpfish try to blend in with rocks and kelp stalks.*

9. **Rocky bottom** *Giant kelps grow only where their holdfasts can attach to a rock-hard bottom.*

10. **Ling cod** *This fierce predator ambushes smaller fish that come into the forest to feed.*

11. **Sea urchin** *Purple sea urchins graze on kelp. They are a favorite food of sea otters.*

Sea level
0 ft (0 m)

30 ft (10 m)

2,000 ft (600 m)

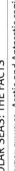

Antarctic diatoms
Diatoms are speck-sized algae that come in many interesting shapes. They are a favorite meal for shrimplike animals called krill.

Seals Several kinds of seals live in the Southern Ocean. Some hunt fish, but the spotted leopard seal also preys on penguins, squid, and other seals.

Antarctic birds
Antarctic birds, such as petrels and fulmars, feed on squid and krill. Skuas steal penguin eggs.

Penguins Penguins are flightless birds found only in the Southern Hemisphere. Like whales and seals, they have a thick layer of fatty blubber to keep them warm.

Emperor penguins
Emperor penguins are the largest penguins. They are much better swimmers than they are walkers, and dive for food.

POLAR SEAS: THE FACTS

LOCATION EXAMPLES: Arctic and Antarctic regions

ANIMALS: Polar bears, walrus, seals, whales, cod, lumpfish, jellies with long tentacles, brittle stars, and bristle worms in the Arctic; seals, penguins, squid, whales, octopus, comb jellies, deep-sea cucumbers, and soft corals in the Antarctic

PLANTS: Diatoms and phytoplankton in both regions, the kelp *Chorda filum* in the Arctic

MAJOR THREATS: Habitat loss, global climate change, pollution

PHOTO: Icy polar seas in the Arctic Ocean

Life in a World of Ice

Polar Seas

Polar seas are at the icy ends of Earth. The North Pole lies in the center of the Arctic Ocean, where deep waters are the coldest on the planet. Only a small number of fish and other sea creatures live or visit there. One of them is the huge sleeper shark, which grows up to 20 feet (6 m) long. Scientists found one of them with a reindeer in its stomach. The Southern Ocean around Antarctica is home to many more species, including penguins, seals, whales, giant squid, billions of thumb-size krill, fish that contain "antifreeze," and sturdy glass sponges.

BREAKING THROUGH THE ICE

An icebreaker is specially built to ram through polar sea ice. The ship's heavy bow does not cut through the ice. Instead, it slides up over the ice and crushes it.

Antennas Antennas receive radio and satellite signals.

Bridge Instruments for navigation and operating the ship are located on the bridge.

Bow Reinforced with extra steel, the bow can withstand the pressure of thick ice.

Hull The hull is broad so that the icebreaker is stable in stormy seas and can ride up on the ice.

Sea spider *Creeping sea spiders look like insects, but they are relatives of crabs.*

The Southern Ocean

The Southern Ocean surrounds Antarctica and the South Pole. Its surface waters are regularly replaced by water welling up from far below. This bottom water contains nutrients for diatoms and small animals that in turn are food for larger sea life.

Killer whales *Killer whales, or orcas, prey on seals, sharks, and other whales.*

Colossal squid *Huge squid can grow more than 66 feet (20 m) long—even larger than sperm whales. They are some of the most amazing creatures in Antarctic seas.*

Blue whale *A blue whale has no teeth. It uses long bristles in its mouth, called baleen, to strain krill from seawater.*

Icebergs *Icebergs can be flat or shaped like small mountains. When an iceberg is taller than it is wide, more than 90 percent of it is submerged underwater.*

Weddell seal *Weddell seals are champion divers. They can stay submerged for up to 15 minutes and may dive to 1,200 feet (400 m) or more.*

Icefish *Icefish have no red blood cells so their blood is clear. Like many other polar animals, icefish have a form of antifreeze in their blood. It acts in the same way that antifreeze prevents water in a car radiator from freezing.*

Comb jellies *Despite their name and see-through bodies, comb jellies are not jellyfish. They belong to a curious group of animals called cnidarians (pronounced ny-DARE-ee-anz).*

Sea cucumber *Spiky sea cucumbers sometimes roam the seafloor in large herds.*

Sea level
0 ft (0 m)

5 ft (1.5 m)

660 ft (200 m)

SUNLIGHT ZONE: THE FACTS

LOCATION EXAMPLES: The upper sunlit region of the whole world ocean beyond the continental shelf

ANIMALS: Blue shark, mako shark, flying fish, mola mola, bluefin tuna, manta ray, mahi mahi, blue whale, giant jellyfish, by-the-wind sailor

PLANTS: Phytoplankton

MAJOR THREATS: Overfishing, pollution, oil spills

PHOTO: School of big-eye trevally, Solomon Islands

Phytoplankton
A single teacupful of sunlit seawater may contain millions of phytoplankton.

Teeming with Life in the
Sunlight Zone

The upper two percent of the world ocean is packed with more life than all the other sea realms put together. Sunlight is the secret to this bounty. Here, microscopic organisms called phytoplankton use sunlight energy to make their own food. These solar-powered food factories fuel a vast ocean food web. Small floating animals, or zooplankton, eat phytoplankton, then are consumed by all sorts of hungry predators—from shrimps the size of a thumbnail to massive whales. Sharks and other large fish hunt here as well, and nothing goes to waste. Sinking leftovers will feed animals in the inky depths below.

Zooplankton *Zooplankton are tiny animals that drift with the currents. Most are hard to see without a microscope.*

Blue whale *Blue whales filter plankton from seawater through comblike bristles called baleen.*

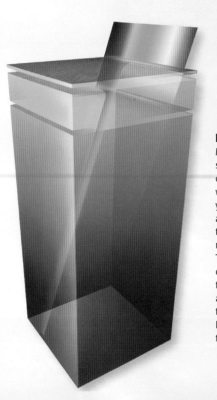

Let there be light
Most ocean creatures need sunlight to survive. Sunlight combines the light of many wavelengths, including red, yellow, green, and blue. Green and blue light travel the deepest through seawater and scatter more than red or yellow light. This is why the ocean looks blue or green. Only blue light reaches the bottom of the sunlight zone, about 660 feet (200 m) beneath the ocean's surface, and beyond. Below 3,300 feet (1,000 m) there is only darkness.

Flying fish *Flying fish jump from the water to escape predators. They use their large pelvic fins to glide through the air before they plunge back into the sea.*

Making food for all

The ocean food web depends on its smallest members, the phytoplankton. Most are only a single cell, but if phytoplankton disappeared, the food web would collapse. For example, during an El Niño event when phytoplankton numbers are reduced, most marine creatures are forced to migrate or die of starvation.

Humans *Humans become part of the ocean food web when they catch and eat seafood. A few large sharks are the only fish that sometimes prey on people.*

Blue shark *Blue sharks travel more of the world ocean than any other kind of shark.*

Mahi mahi *"Mahi" is a Hawaiian word that means "strong." Mahi mahi are a popular food fish for humans.*

Oceanic white tip shark *These large tropical sharks usually eat fish but may attack shipwrecked humans drifting in the ocean.*

Mola mola *A mola mola can grow to more than 3,300 pounds (1,500 kg)—as heavy as a black rhinoceros. Mola molas have a flattened body and loll at the surface, eating large plankton.*

Bluefin tuna *Schools of bluefin tuna chase after schools of squid and small fish.*

Sea level
0 ft (0 m)

660 ft (200 m)

30,000 ft (10,000 m)

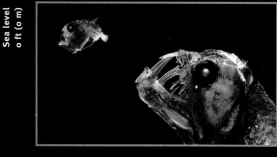

DEEP SEA: THE FACTS

LOCATION EXAMPLES: Worldwide in the ocean realm from 660 feet (200 m) to 30,000 feet (10,000 m)

ANIMALS: Flashlight fish, giant squid, viperfish, oarfish, red prawn, scaly dragonfish, and cookiecutter shark in the twilight zone; gulper eel, anglerfish, slickhead, deep-sea rattail, and deep-sea sea star in the dark zone

PLANTS: None

MAJOR THREATS: Pollution, global climate change

PHOTO: Viperfish chasing a hatchetfish in the deep sea

Creatures of the
Deep Sea

About 660 feet (200 m) under the surface, the eerie realm of the deep ocean begins. Here, the fish are small but fierce predators, with large eyes and mouths and spiky teeth. Many fish, squid, and shrimps in these murky depths are bioluminescent—they have glowing organs that beam out a deep-sea light show. Deeper still, below about 3,300 feet (1,000 m), some of the oddest fish in the sea live in total darkness and under crushing water pressure. Their bodies are soft and squishy, and curving fangs fill their huge, gaping mouths. Many are blind. Some fish lure prey with their light organs, while others hunt using their keen senses of smell and touch.

Lanternfish *The large eyes of a lanternfish help it see in the dim middle depths. Each lanternfish species has a different pattern of light organs on its sides.*

Rattail fish *A long, tapering tail gives rattail fish their name.*

Blue hake *Blue hakes have a keen sense of hearing, but no one has discovered what they listen to in the depths.*

THE DEPTHS: NOT JUST FOR FISH

Fish are not the only creatures in the deep sea. Invertebrates, such as jellyfish, sea stars, and amphipods also live in the ocean's depths. Some have light organs or are brightly colored. Others are as transparent as glass.

Deep-sea amphipod Most amphipods are smaller than a fingernail.

Soft coral Some soft corals live as deep as 10,000 feet (3,000 m) under the surface.

Sea star Green-glowing light organs outline the arms of this deep-sea sea star.

Coronate medusa This relative of jellyfish emits flashes of blue light. It feeds on small swimming crustaceans and organic particles floating in the ocean's depths.

Glowing lure
The anglerfish's bright lure attracts predatory fish that hope to capture it. Instead, the predatory fish become meals for the anglerfish.

Deep-sea anglerfish
This illustration shows a female deep-sea anglerfish. Males are only about the size of a small marble.

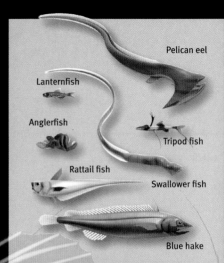

Pelican eel

Lanternfish

Anglerfish

Tripod fish

Rattail fish

Swallower fish

Blue hake

Comparisons of the deep
Some deep-sea fish are as small as your thumb; others have long, snakelike bodies. The pelican eel and swallower fish measure more than two feet (0.6 m) long. Both have large jaws that open wide to capture prey.

Attached male
The tiny male anglerfish lives attached to the female.

Down deep, up close
It takes a lot of food to fuel a large body, so in the deep sea, where food is scarce, most fish are small. The deep-sea anglerfish (above) is only five or six inches (13 cm) long. But in spite of the challenges of finding food and immense water pressure, a few fish survive more than 27,000 feet (8,370 m) under the surface—this is more than five times deeper than the Grand Canyon, in the USA.

Tripod fish *A tripod fish is about as long as a hot dog. It perches near the bottom on its long tail and pectoral fins.*

Sea level 0 ft (0 m)

660 ft (200 m)

36,100 ft (11,022 m)

OCEAN FLOOR: THE FACTS

LOCATION EXAMPLES: The seafloor from the edge of the continental shelf all the way down to the dark abyss

ANIMALS: Giant tube worms, white clams, crabs, shrimp, sea spiders, and eelpout live around vents and smokers; herds of brittle stars, feather stars, burrowing urchins, sea pens, and glass sponges live away from vents

PLANTS: None

MAJOR THREATS: Pollution, such as ocean dumping

PHOTO: Tiny crabs around a hot hydrothermal vent

Life on the Ocean Floor

Hot Vents

At cracks in the seafloor where Earth's crustal plates form, a scalding soup of chemicals spews from undersea hot springs called hydrothermal vents. Here and there, some of the chemicals build up into towering "smokers" that spout jets of gray or black water. Communities of strange animals live around the vents—giant tube worms with blood-red plumes of tentacles, huge clams and mussels, hairy white crabs, and leggy sea spiders. Since the first hot vents were discovered, deep-sea researchers have found dozens more of them.

Exploring the deep sea

In 1977, scientists in the submersible *Alvin* were amazed to discover hydrothermal vents near the equator off South America. The vents were 8,200 feet (2,500 m) below the surface. *Alvin*'s mechanical arm took samples of tube worms and other vent creatures for study.

Rock chimney *Minerals in the water harden into rock chimneys that can be more than 63 feet (19 m) high.*

Eelpout *Slim, eel-like fish called eelpouts prey on other members of the vent community, such as crabs and amphipods.*

Giant tube worms *Giant tube worms can be up to eight feet (2.4 m) tall. These huge worms never need to eat because bacteria in their bodies convert vent water chemicals into food.*

Super submersible *Alvin has room for two scientists and a pilot. It can go as deep as 14,764 feet (4,500 m).*

Monster mussels *Like tube worms, the huge mussels of vent communities are "fed" by bacteria that live in their flesh.*

Brittle stars *Brittle stars use their long, jointed arms to grasp objects.*